Affirmations from a Hospice Patient Named JOB

"Shall we accept good from
God, and not trouble?"
Job 2:10 (NIV)

Chaplain Lonnie Royal, Sr.

Forward by Eliza L. Royal

ISBN (978-0-9719914-5-3)
Breicha Publishing Services
www.brendajoycenichols.com

Printed in U.S.A.
First Printing 2020

DEDICATION

In memory of all those individuals who have walked through a Job experience, death of a loved one, divorce, a personal serious illness, or any of the traumas of life, and survived to bring hope to others.

PREFACE

A ll believers in Christ, God, and the Bible can take courage.

"We want you to know what happens to the believers who have died, so you will not grieve like people who have no hope."

"We believe that Jesus died and was raised to life again. We also believe that when he returns, God will bring back with him believers who have died."

(I Thessalonians 4:13-14)

"For we don't live for ourselves or die for ourselves. If we live, it's to honor the Lord, and if we die, it's to honor the Lord. So, whether we live or die, we belong to the Lord. Christ died and rose again for this very purpose to be Lord both of the living and the dead."

(Romans 14:7-9)

FORWARD

The last five years have been traumatic for me. I have had to face the reality of death and dying. My father, my sister Alberta and her husband, my sister Bobbie and her husband Mike, my oldest brother, and my mother. Each death brought an evaluation of my own life and relationship with the deceased individual.

Recently, my younger brother had several strokes and needed assisted living. As the oldest, a lot of responsibility and personal strength was required to maintain stability and peace in my life. I was also the most financially stable of my siblings and spent a great deal of my own personal assets.

As a result, I began to have physical problems and anxiety. My husband, a Chaplain, recommended several books in his extensive library. My daughter enrolled us in a Grief Recovery Program at a hospital. My husband also gave me scriptures from the book of Job that related all the adversity Job had experienced, endured, and conquered.

I was surprised to see myself in the pages of these books. I was also grateful as "quietness and confidence" entered my heart, mind, and soul. I was empowered with renewed strength. The heaviness in my heart lifted and I felt alive again.

It is my belief that this little book can help heal a broken, battered, and bruised soul. I know that it helped my own broken heart to heal.

~ Eliza L. Royal ~

INTRODUCTION

King Hezekiah became deathly ill and the prophet Isaiah was sent to visit him. He gave the king this message: *"This is what the Lord says: Set your affairs in order, for you are going to die. You shall not recover from this illness."*

"When Hezekiah heard this, he turned his face to the wall and prayed to the Lord. Then he broke down and wept bitterly." (II Kings 19:1-3) The Lord heard his prayer, saw his tears, and gave him fifteen (15) more years of life.

There is much to be said about getting our house (affairs) in order before we die. The sooner the better. We have modern examples of celebrities who didn't, and their estates are still in limbo (Aretha Franklin, Prince, and James Brown are among them). Even if someone commits suicide, it is good practice to have one's affairs in order.

"When Ahithophel *(a counselor who advised Absalom, King David's son, to kill David)* realized that his advice had not been followed, he saddled his donkey, went to his hometown, set his affairs in order, and hanged himself. He died there and was buried in the family tomb." (II Samuel 17:23)

For many death is an unwelcomed enemy. There are some who have lived a full life and welcome death. There are others who have suffered much through sickness, disease, or life itself, and prefer death.

TABLE OF CONTENTS

Spiritual Presence and Silence 1

Kindness to a Fainting Friend 3

Leave Me Alone 4

A Few Days 5

I Know a Few Things 6

Please Be Silent 7

Let Me Speak 9

The Length of My Days...................................... 11

I Would Encourage You...................................... 12

Where Is My Hope? 13

Where Is My Family?.. 15

Why Should I Pray? 16

Consider Your Clichés 18

Caring, Comforting, or Critical 19

The Years Behind Me 21

A Long Good Life.. 23

Smile at the Discouraged 25

Hello and Goodbye 26

Affirmation 28

Seasons of Our Life.. 29

Additional Theology from Job.............................. 30

Epilogue 32

Bibliography.. 34

About the Author 36

> **❝** *Engage in the ministry of spiritual presence and being present through silence.* **❞**

"Job's friends traveled from their homes to comfort and console him. They scarcely recognized him…. They sat with him seven days and nights. No one said a word to Job, for they saw his suffering was too great for words."

(Job 2:11-13)

In times of distress many people are reluctant to visit with those in distress. They fear they will say or do the wrong thing and make things worse. People rarely remember what we say. What they most remember is that we were there. Familiar faces offer strength beyond description. Often, the best comfort is the gift of presence and just being there. Again, "Having you there makes a difference, just having you there."

> ### *Having you there makes a difference!*

1

"When I was in seminary", a minister said, "I thought I would have all these profound things to say to someone whose spouse had left them or whose child had died.

But I've learned that what people really want is for you to say, *"Oh, that's terrible. I'm so sorry.* **And, sit there and listen."**

(Romans 12:14) tells us, "don't think you know it all. Be happy with those who are happy and weep with those who weep."

> *Be happy with those who are happy*
> *and weep with those who weep!*

" **Be kind to a fainting friend.** "

"Don't I have the right to complain?"
"My appetite disappears when I look at it,"
"I gag at the thought of eating it,"
"Oh, that I might have my request,"
"That God would grant my desire,"
"I wish he would reach out his hand and kill me."
"But I don't have the strength to endure."
"I have nothing to live for."
"Do I have the strength of a stone?"
"Is my body made of bronze?"
"No, I am utterly helpless,"
"Without any chance of success."
"One should be kind to a fainting friend."

(Job 6:5-14)

When our bodies stop craving food and water **("my appetite disappears")** and our organs start shutting down (including stoppage of urination), we are in a danger zone.

> *It could also signal we are approaching the end of life.*

"Some were fools; they rebelled and suffered for their sins. They couldn't stand the thought of food and were knocking on death's door. 'Lord, help!' they cried in their trouble, and he saved them from their distress. He sent out his word and healed them, snatching them from the door of death."

(Psalm 107:17-20)

3

" *Please leave me alone for my few remaining days.* "

"I hate my life and don't want to go on living."

"Oh, leave me alone for my few remaining days."

"What are people that you should make so much of us?"

"For you examine us every moment."
"Why won't you leave me alone?"

"At least long enough for me to swallow!"

(Job 7: 16-19)

(Isolation and Depression – Stages of Dying)

Elijah *(Old Testament prophet)* fled for his life. He went alone into the wilderness, traveling all day. He sat under a solitary tree and prayed that he might die.

> **"I have had enough, Lord," he said. "Take my life, for I am no better than my ancestors who have already died."** *(I Kings 19:4)*

4

66   *I have only a few days left,*
so, leave me alone.   99

"I have only a few days left, so leave me alone, that I may have a moment of comfort."

(Job 10:20 & 21)

Isolation!

"So, leave me alone"
**is a natural, normal and expected
stage of grief and dying.**

Some have experienced being by a loved one's bedside 24/7. The moment they took a break and returned to the bedside, their loved one had died. It was as if the dying person waited to be alone to pass on.

" *Who does not know these things you are saying?* "

"You people really know everything, don't you?"
"And when you die, wisdom will die with you!"
"Well, I know a few things myself. "

The dying as teachers.

"And you're no better than I am."
"Who doesn't know these things you've been saying?'
(Job 12:2 & 3-13:2)

The dying often know they are dying.

Patronization
(telling them you're ok or you're not dying)
may offend them.

6

" *If only you could be silent.* "

"If only you could be silent!
That's the wisest thing you could do.
Listen to my charge.
Pay attention to my arguments."

(Job 13:5 & 6)

"Listen closely to what I am saying. That's one consolation you can give me. Bear with me and let me speak. After I have spoken, you may resume."

(Job 21:2-3)

Sometimes with grieving, sick and dying patients it is important:

- *To be silent.*

- *Listen until they finish talking and are silent.*

- *Listening is consoling and affirming.*

7

The grieving, sick and dying will appreciate and find fulfillment in being listened to and being heard. This will empower them to share their feelings freely.

Joyce Huggett in her book *"Listening to Others"* writes how she has been thanked for all she has done, when she has not done anything but be present and listen.

May the Lord help us to listen, sense other's feelings and needs and respond appropriately.

" *Be silent now and leave me alone! Let me speak, and I will face the consequences.* "

"Your platitudes are as valuable as ashes.
Be silent now and leave me alone.
Let me speak, and I will face the consequences.
Yes, I will take my life in my hands
And say what I really think.
God may kill me, but I have no other hope.
I am going to argue my case with him.
But this is what will save me- I am not Godless.
If I were, I could not stand before him.
Listen closely to what I am about to say,
Hear me out."

(Job 13:12-17)

Silence, Isolation, bargaining with God, and faith in being right with God is important.

> During the most difficult stages of life, many find comfort in their faith ("But this is what will save me, *I am not Godless*, if I were, I could not stand before God.")

"We teach and counsel each other with the wisdom Christ gives. We avoid ruining our lives, instead we allow ourselves to be filled with the Holy Spirit by "Singing psalms, hymns and spiritual songs among ourselves, and making music to the Lord in our hearts. We give Thanks continually to God."

(Ephesians 5:18-20 and Colossians 3:16-17)

> ## *You, oh Lord, have decided the length of our days.* ,,

"You have decided the length of our lives.
You know how many months we will live.
And we are not given a minute longer.
When people die, their strength is gone.
They breathe their last."

(Job 14:5, 6, 10)

Many hospice patients of all or no faith believe that there is given to us a certain number of years to live.

"You have decided the length of our lives." The days of our lives are threescore and ten (70 years) and if by reason of strength fourscore (80 years) ...and we end our lives with a sigh."

(Psalm 90:9-10)

"You saw me before I was born. Every day of my life was recorded in your book. Every moment was laid out before a single day had passed."

(Psalm 139:16)

"It is appointed for all men once to die and after that the judgment."

(Hebrews 9:27) (KJV)

" But, if it was me, I would encourage you. "

"I have heard all of this before. What miserable comforters you are! Won't you ever stop blowing hot air? What makes you keep on talking? I could say the same things if you were in my place. But if it were me, I would encourage you, I would try to take away your grief."

(Job 16:2-5)

A short life review could help a patient find meaning to their life and their death. Review of life accomplishments, joys, careers, family memories, memories of travel and special events will prove helpful.

Enjoying Life — A Gift from God!

Words of Solomon, known as the wisest person that ever lived; "Here is what I have seen to be good; it is appropriate to eat, drink, and experience satisfaction in all of life and work, during the short life God has given. This is a gift from God. When we enjoy our work and accept our lot in life, God keeps us so busy enjoying life that we don't have time to brood over the past."

(Ecclesiastes 5-18-20)

" *Where is my hope?* "

"My days are over.
My hope has disappeared.
My heart's desires are broken.
These men say that night is day;
They claim that the darkness is light.
What if I go to the grave?
And make my bed in darkness?
What if I call the grave my father?
And the maggot my mother or my sister?
Where is my hope?
Can anyone find it?
No, my hope will go down with me to the grave.
We will rest together in the dust!"

(Job 17:11-16)

What affirmation can be given to an agnostic, *an atheist or non-believer?*

"No, my hope will go down with me to the grave."
This is Old Testament (OT) theology. New Testament (NT) theology says;

**"If our hope in Christ is only for this
life, we are more to be pitied than anyone
in the world…. Those who
have died will be raised
to life forever."**

(I Corinthians 15:19 & 52)

"We are not alone; we live in God's world. We believe in God: who has created and is creating, who has come in Jesus, the Word made flesh.

In life, in death, in life beyond death, God is with us. We are not alone. Thanks be to God."

*(Affirmation of faith from the
United Church of Canada)*

" *My family is gone!* "

"My relatives stay far away,
And my friends have turned against me.
My family is gone,
And my close friends have forgotten me.
My breath is repulsive to my wife.
I am rejected by my own family.
I have been reduced to skin and bones
And have escaped death by the skin of my teeth.
For the hand of God has struck me."

(Job 19: 13-21)

"Before I was afflicted, I went astray."

(Psalm 119:67)- (KJV)

**How do we respond to the belief
God has put this disease on the patient?**

**Or, that we bring sickness and disease
upon ourselves?**

**When a patient's breath is repulsive
how do we react? Hopefully with
compassion and understanding.**

" *What will it do us to pray?* "

(Job 21:15)

How is prayer affirming?
How will we know when to pray?
Or, if we are to pray?

Jesus taught, "we are always to pray and never give up." (Luke 18:1) He gave us the model prayer (The Lord's Prayer or The Our Father Prayer).

(Matthew 6:9-13)

James, a leader of the early church taught,
"We pray whenever we are troubled."

(James 5:13)

Books from Phillip Yancey. *"Prayer Does It Really Help"* and *"Where is God When It Hurts"*; and, *"Praying Our Goodbyes"* by Joyce Rupp; and *"Standing in the Circle of Grief"* by Blair Gilmer Meeks answer Job's question:

It is to be noted the person grieving or dying may not be able themselves to pray or may have difficulty finding the words to say.

Put words to your sorrow and grief,

"Give sorrow words; the grief that does not speak knits up the o-er wrought heart and bids it break."
(William Shakespeare - Macbeth)

The Holy Bible encourages us, "Don't worry about anything; instead pray about everything. Tell God what you need and thank God for all he has done. Then you will experience God's peace, which exceeds anything we can understand. His peace will guard your hearts and minds as you live in Christ Jesus."

(Philippians 4:6-7)

" *How can your empty clichés comfort me?* "

Watch clichés! We all profit from our one liners affirmation of faith;

"This too will pass."
"I am taking things one day at a time."
"I can do all things through Christ who strengthens me."
"Into each life a little rain must fall,"
"God does not make mistakes" . . . and so on.

> Cliché's like –
> **"God needed another angel"**
> may not be comforting to a parent
> whose child has just died.

As stated previously, saying, "I'm so sorry," and "that's awful" may be more appropriate. **Then, provide spiritual presence with silence**.

This will provide opportunity for our loved one to express their own faith or theology, which we can affirm.

" *Whose spirit speaks through you?* "

- *Caring spirit*
- *Comforting spirit*
- *Critical spirit*

"Where have you gotten all these wise sayings? Whose spirit speaks through you?"

(Job 26:4)

Be careful about spouting our own agenda or theology without being asked or given permission.

Loved ones will ask the question why. One question very difficult to answer is, **"Why did God take my child, my wife, husband, son or daughter?**

> **Maybe the quality of life matters as much as the quantity of life.**

19

King David, upon the death of his infant, responded; "I fasted and wept (he also laid on the ground) while the child was alive. For I said, perhaps the Lord will be gracious and let the child live. He is dead. I will go to him one day, but he cannot return to me."

(II Samuel 12:15-24)

We can comfort each other when we have done all we can.

" *I long for the years gone by. . .* "

"I long for the years gone by when God took care of me, and I walked safely through the darkness. The young stepped aside when they saw me. And even the aged rose in respect at my coming. All who heard me praised me. All who saw me spoke well of me."

(Job 29:1-11)

Affirm, respect and honor each person. Give and maintain each person's dignity and pride.

Plato once said, "Be kind, for everyone you meet is fighting a battle."

Strong confidence and faith may wane during crisis, sickness and as we approach death. It is normal, natural and to be expected. At this point courage is needed.

The Lord told Gideon (a leader and Judge over his people), "Go in the strength you have...and I will be with you."

(Judges 6:14-16)

"Courage is fear that has said it's prayers and moves forward. Let the road be rough and dreary, and its end far out of sight, foot it bravely strong or weary."

(by Dorothy Bernard, an American actress)

21

Be strong and take courage, for the Lord will go before you and God's light will show the way. The one who lives within you will be strong in you today.

So, remember, **"Courage is fear that has said its prayers and moves forward."**

"If you can't fly – run.
If you can't run – walk.
If you can't walk – crawl.
But whatever you do,
you must keep moving forward."

Dr. Martin Luther King, Jr.

" *I thought . . .*
after a long, good life. . . "

"I thought, surely, I will die surrounded by my family after a long, good life."

(Job 29: 18)

How do we affirm such a patient if family isn't supportive, their life is cut short and they feel all alone?

Be ready to encourage lonely loved ones to identify living family members (sister, brother, aunt, uncle, cousins or even neighbors). Help them make the connection.

> **As we share information and have conversation with patients, family members and friends, let us not forget to talk about pets.**

As I have looked around in a patient's room, I have seen pictures of the family pet. As a hospice chaplain, I have had to accept and honor the presence of two or three humongous furry family members. God loves us humans with an everlasting love. God loves and cares about animals also.

In Jonah 4:11- The Lord said, "Should not I care about the great city of Nineveh as well as the animals?" Pets are God's creation that provide unconditional love. Let's remember pets have names, living quarters and are family too.

Be assured, "God places the lonely (solitary) in families."
(Psalm 68:6)

Instead of being surrounded by his children, all of Job's children died. Many parents have this experience and like Job it breaks their hearts.

Show compassion and empathy when people share the death of their children. Say something like. "your daughter died when she was eight years old?"

Then be quiet and listen.

" *When they were discouraged, I smiled...* "

"When they were discouraged, I smiled at them. My look of approval was precious to them."

(Job 29: 24)

In everyday life and professionally, we try to maintain a smile. We can turn a frown upside down by smiling. (From Positive Promotion 8 Ways to Stay Positive)

[1] "Simply Smile: A smile has great power to boost your mood as well as lift the spirits of others."
[8] "Show the way: Present a positive attitude. Your enthusiasm will spread, brightening everyone's day."

> **With everyone we can share**
> **Job's wisdom:**
> **"Smile at the discouraged."**
> **"Look with approval at others."**

Our countenance can express compassion, sorrow, or joy as we take our lead from those we encounter.

WE ARE CONSTANTLY SAYING HELLO AND GOODBYE

(by Joyce Rupp)

After every goodbye there is a hello to the new. Letting go and carrying on can be hard work and takes time. Joyce Rupp in her book, "Praying Our Goodbyes," suggests we pray our goodbyes using scriptures. Her book is "a spiritual companion though life's losses and sorrows." She discovered one-liners can be helpful with our challenge . . .

> *"Expect the unexpected."*
> *"This too will pass."*
> *"I'm taking it one day at a time."*
> *"All will be well in the end."*
> *"Be good to yourself."*
> *"God can cause all things to work together for the good."*
> *"It is what it is."*

When our favorite one-liner no longer works for us, adopt a new one.

We get attached to co-workers, patients, family, relationship, homes, cars, pets and on and on. Change, however, is inevitable. The sooner we understand and accept the hello/goodbye pattern, the better we will be able to cope with whatever life throws at us.

Seasons change, we fall back and spring forward as time changes. Tree leaves are green and then turn brown. Leaves fall to the ground as seasons change or bud to proclaim the beginning of another season.

Truly, truly the words of scripture and the lyrics of a song by the Eagles are helpful, *"Change, change, for everything under the sun, there is a time and season."*

Things happen. It is what it is. What is it we are saying hello to and what must we joyfully or painfully say goodbye to? Let us practice letting go and trusting God to turn our goodbyes and hellos into a new and living way.

Having difficulties with hello's and goodbyes?

EAP, Social Workers, Case Managers, Pastors, or Chaplains are available to assist with the journey.

AFFIRMATION

A declaration that something is true. A positive assertion based on facts. Negative declaration or assertion by patient based on facts or their personal faith can be affirmed or acknowledged? Something noteworthy.

Elisabeth Kubler-Ross book, "On Death and Dying" (what the dying teach doctors, nurses, clergy, and their families), identifies 5 stages of dying:

First Stage: Denial and Isolation

Second Stage: Anger

Third Stage: Bargaining (Abraham)
Gen. 18:23-33

Fourth Stage: Depression

Fifth Stage: Acceptance

What affirmation can we give at each stage?

Scenario: A patient or loved one tells you, "I am tired and want to go to sleep. I don't feel like talking with you now."

Possible Affirmation: Respect their wishes and be there for the primary care giver (PCG) and family.

"For everything there is a season,
A time for every activity under heaven.
A time to be born and a time to die.
A time to plant and a time to harvest.
A time to kill and a time to heal.
A time to tear down and a time to build up.
A time to cry and a time to laugh.
A time to grieve and a time to dance.
A time to scatter stones and,
A time to gather stones.
A time to embrace and,
A time to refrain from embracing.
A time to search and a time to quit searching.
A time to keep and a time to throw away.
A time to tear and a time to mend.
A time to be quiet and a time to speak.
A time to love and a time to hate.
A time for war and a time for peace.

Yet, *God has made everything beautiful for its own time.
God has planted eternity in the human heart, but even so,
people cannot see the whole scope of God's work from
beginning to end."*   (Ecclesiastes 3:1-8 & 11)

> *"While I thought that I was learning how to
> live, I have been learning how to die."*
> ~Leonardo Da Vince~

ADDITIONAL THEOLOGY FROM JOB

"Naked I came from my mother's womb, and naked I will leave this life, the Lord gives, and the Lord takes away, blessed be the name the Lord."

(Job 1:21)

"Should we accept only good from God and not adversity?"

(Job 2:10)

"Though He slay me, I will trust him."

(Job 13:15)

"All of the days of my appointed time will I wait, until my change comes."

(Job 14:14)

"I know that my redeemer liveth and he shall stand at last on the earth. And after my skin is destroyed, this I know, that in my flesh I shall see God. Whom I shall see for myself and my eyes shall behold, and not another. How my heart yearns within me."

(Job 19:25)

"I had heard rumors about you, but now my eyes have seen you. Therefore, I take back my words and repent in dust and ashes."

(Job 42:5, 6)

"After Job had prayed for his friends, the Lord restored his prosperity and doubled his possessions. . .his brothers, sisters and former acquaintances came. . .and offered him sympathy and comfort."

(Job 42: 10, 11)

Could it be the best is yet to come in our lives?

No matter our age, maybe there is much more to see and experience. Hold on and don't give up. Have faith in God. For all the trouble you have been through, God is able to give you double for your trouble.

> **The bottom line is,**
>
> **"God will care for us every day."**

"Be not dismayed whatever betides,
God will take care of you.
Beneath His wings of love abide,
God will take care of you.
God will take care of you,
thro' every day, o'er all the way.
He will take care of you;
God will take care of you."

*(From the song- "God will take care of you"
by Civilla D. Martin)*

From Saint Francis De Sales: "Do not fear what may happen tomorrow. The same loving God who cares for you today will care for you tomorrow and every day. Either God will shield you from suffering, or God will give you unfailing strength to bear it. Be at peace, and put aside all anxious thoughts, worrying or imaginings." God will care for us today, tomorrow and forever more.

"And after you have suffered a little while, the God of all grace will himself complete and make you what you ought to be. God will establish and ground you securely, strengthen and settle you."

(I Peter 5:10)

Now, "You have heard of the endurance, (the patience and suffering) of Job; and you have seen the Lord's purpose and how God richly blessed him in the end."
 (James 5:11)

BIBLIOGRAPHY OF RESOURCES

Didion, Joan; The Year of Magical Thinking and The Book of Common Prayer

Dunn, Hank; Hard Choices for Loving People (When to remove life support and feeding tubes).

Gunderson, Gary; Five Leading Causes of Life (How to have the best quality of life possible).

Huggett, Joyce; Listening to Others (in order to hear their hearts and respond effectively).

Kubler-Ross, Elisabeth, MD.; On Death and Dying (What the Dying Have to Teach Doctors, Nurses, Clergy, and Their Families.)

Lutzer, Erwin W.; One Minute After You Die

Meeks, Blair Gilmer; Standing in the Circle of Grief (Prayers, including one for removal of life support).

Reimer, Lawrence D. and James T. Wagner; The Hospital Handbook (The book on Clergy visitation).

Rosenberg, Marshall B. PHD; Nonviolent Communication (A Language of Life).

Rupp, Joyce; Praying Our Goodbyes (Using Scripture).

Westberg, Granger; Good Grief (10 Steps for "good grief" and finding a new normal).

Yancey, Phillips; Where is God When It Hurts? (Address issues of pain and suffering).

Yancey, Phillips; Prayer. Does it Help? (compiled true stories, prayers and insight).

ABOUT THE AUTHOR

Chaplain Lonnie Royal, Sr. served as a Casualty Assistance Officer in the military. He assisted in the notification of next of kin, in the death of servicemen, and women.

He served as pastor of two United Methodist Churches and as Parish Director over six (6) churches.

He later served four (4) years with Gilchrist Hospice, in Baltimore, MD, as a Baltimore Regional Hospice Chaplain.

He recently served five (5) years as HealthSouth/ Encompass North Rehabilitation Hospital Chaplain, in Memphis, TN.

He is a retired United Methodist Elder devoting time as a husband, father, writer and apologetic.